Do You KNOW?™

THE GREEN BAY PACKERS

A hard-hitting quiz for tailgaters, referee-haters, armchair quarterbacks, and anyone who'd kill for their team

Guy Robinson

SOURCEBOOKS, INC.®
NAPERVILLE, ILLINOIS

Published by Sourcebooks, Inc.
P.O. Box 4410, Naperville, Illinois 60567-4410
(630) 961-3900
Fax: (630) 961-2168
www.sourcebooks.com

Printed and bound in the United States of America
SP 10 9 8 7 6 5 4 3 2 1

This is the kind of quiz that will make you dig deep into the football compartment of your brain. If you *really* know the Packers and their history, you'll be able to answer questions about classic games you were lucky enough to see while they happened, historic series you've watched on DVD, and unbelievable plays you've heard about so often you've come to think you were on the field yourself. You'll know about winning coaches and losing coaches, celebrated passers and legendary runners, thrilling playoff games and enduring records, special rivalries and favorite traditions—the stuff of countless game days and time afterward sitting around arguing about whether he ever should've gone for the Hail Mary and whose defense was *really* impenetrable.

You should find that some of the answers pop readily to mind. Others will be a true challenge. And however good you think you are, you can expect to face a few that will stop you cold. That's part of the fun.

So here are 100 questions. Count ten points for each correct answer. Where a question has more than one part, you'll be told how to divide the credit. Here and there you'll find a chance to earn five or ten bonus points, so it's theoretically possible to score more than 1,000. (But you won't!)

Figure your performance this way:

Above 900:	**Spectacular!**
700–899:	A very solid showing.
500–699:	Nothing to be ashamed of.
Below 500:	Told you it was tough.

1. Who was George Whitney Calhoun?

   _____

2. Pick the correct nickname for the city of Green Bay:

   a. "Cheese City, America"
   b. "Titletown USA"
   c. "Home of the Champs"
   d. "Wisconsin's Finest"

3. The Packers once won the National Football League championship *twice* in one year. Explain.

   _____

   _____

4. Who raised some eyebrows during an exhibition game before the 1980 season when he was caught sitting on the bench munching a hot dog while his teammates were being shut out by the Denver Broncos 38–0?

   E_____ J_____

5. Curly Lambeau guided the Packers for an astonishing 31 seasons. Two other head coaches are tied for second-longest reign, nine seasons each. One is Vince Lombardi. Who's the other?

   a. Dan Devine   c. Mike Holmgren
   b. Forrest Gregg   d. Bart Starr

6. And can you name the two head coaches who held the post for just one year? (Hint: It's a pair of Rays.)

   Ray _____ (1958)

   Ray _____ (1999)

7. One of the Rays in the question above did his time between two coaches named Mike. Name the two coaching Mikes.

Mike _____ (1992–98)

Mike _____ (2000–05)

8. He was a Packers draft choice out of the University of Washington in 1993, but he played little in Green Bay, moving on to a better performance with other NFL teams. Need a little more? He's a southpaw quarterback. Now, name him.

M_____ B_____

9. What Packer was first to do the Lambeau Leap, celebrating his touchdown by jumping into the arms of fans in the end zone seats?

L_____ B_____

10. And what team member wrote and recorded a rap song about the Leap? (Five bonus points for the song's title.)

_____

11. Each of these statements about Vince Lombardi is true…except one. Pick the *false* statement.

    a. He usually wore a suit, tie, overcoat, and hat to games.
    b. He never had a losing season with the Packers.
    c. He also head coached the Washington Redskins and New York Giants.
    d. The year after he died, he was elected to the Pro Football Hall of Fame.
    e. U.S. Route 41, as it passes Lambeau Field, is called Lombardi Avenue.

12. When the Packers won the Super Bowl in January 1997 it was the team's first in _____ years.

13. Alone among NFL franchises, Green Bay Packers, Inc., is a publicly owned company. About how many shareholders own a piece of it?

a. 10,000

b. 100,000

c. 750,000

d. 1,500,000

14. Since 1961, the Packers helmet has sported what for a logo?

a. The letter *G* in an oval

b. Lowercase letters *gb*

c. A script *P*

d. A map of Wisconsin with a star at Green Bay

15. What do you call a fan wearing a slab of yellow foam as a hat?

_____

16. In the pre-Favre era, which Packer racked up the most 300-yard passing games? (Ten extra points if you know how many games.)

L_____ D_____

17. This former Packers star didn't use his full first and middle names, Bryan Bartlett. He went with something a little easier on the ear:

_____

18. Under Coach Vince Lombardi, the Packers' signature play was known as:

a. "49 to 4 and Push"

b. "Down They Go"

c. "The Packer Sweep"

d. "Vince's Favorite"

19. For five points each, complete the names of these Green Bay dining establishments owned by former Packers:

a. _____'s Steakhouse
b. _____'s #63 Bar & Grill

20. What team did the Packers shut out in the NFL championship contests of 1939 and 1961? (Ten bonus points for each game score you can give.)

_____

21. Tony Mandarich, a 1989 draft pick who didn't work out all that well, came to Green Bay from:

a. Cornell
b. Alabama
c. Michigan State
d. Minnesota

22. Vince Lombardi's first game as Packers chief was against archrival Chicago. Did he win or lose? (Ten bonus points if you can give the score.)

_____

23. Which of these Packers head coaches never played for the team?

a. Curly Lambeau
b. Bart Starr
c. Forrest Gregg
d. Mike Sherman

24. **What was the original name of Lambeau Field?**
    a. Green Bay Central Park
    b. Packer Stadium
    c. City Stadium
    d. Lambeau Field

25. **Whose ankle injury jump-started Brett Favre's career as a Packer, in a game that ended with a Favre-led storybook comeback? (Five bonus points for naming the opposing team in that first game, ten more for the score.)**

    _____

26. **What sack specialist garnered almost as much attention toward the end of his career for his religious activities and rants against homosexuality as for his defense on the football field?**

    R_____ W_____

27. **What did the Packers do in 1967 that they had also done in 1931? (Hint: No other team has done it even once.)**

    _____

28. **As a favorite target of Brett Favre, Antonio Freeman performed skillfully, reliably, and occasionally acrobatically and breathtakingly. For five points apiece:**
    a. In the Super Bowl XXXI win over the Patriots, how long was the then-record TD pass he caught to put the Packers in the lead? (Come within three yards and you've got your points.) _____
    b. In a game played on November 6, 2000, his much-discussed freakish play of an almost-intercepted Favre pass—miraculously corralling the ball on his back on the wet turf, then executing a quick juke and dashing to the end zone—gave Green Bay an overtime win. Against…?

    _____

29. **Which U.S. president was offered a tryout by the Packers as well as the Detroit Lions?**

   a. Richard Nixon
   b. Gerald Ford
   c. Jimmy Carter
   d. Bill Clinton

30. **Two practice fields in Green Bay are named for former Packers who spent their entire pro careers with the team. Both men are Pro Football Hall of Famers. Five points for each one.**

   C_____ H_____ (1932–41)

   R_____ N_____ (1958–72)

31. **What name is commonly applied to the NFL Championship game played on New Year's Eve 1967, when Green Bay beat Dallas 21–17 as the Fahrenheit thermometer read 13 degrees below zero?**

   _____

32. **Who provided the key blocks for Bart Starr's winning quarterback sneak in that game? Five points for each of the two.**

   K_____ B_____

   J_____ K_____

33. **Of this list, just one didn't play in that championship contest—he joined the team a bit later. Who?**

   a. Forrest Gregg
   b. Willie Wood
   c. Henry Jordan
   d. Willie Davis
   e. Fred Carr
   f. Ray Nitschke

34. **And after that chilly encounter, what did fans start to call Lambeau Field?**

   "_____"

35. **For two points each, match the quote with the Packer who said it:**

   a. "Football is more mental than physical, no matter how it looks from the stands."
   b. "When it's third and ten, you can take the milk drinkers and I'll take the whisky drinkers every time"
   c. "Lombardi treats us all the same—like dogs."
   d. "This is the best place for guys to come and focus on nothing but football."
   e. "If you aren't fired with enthusiasm, you'll be fired—with enthusiasm!"

   f. Vince Lombardi
   g. Max McGee
   h. Brett Favre
   i. Ray Nitschke
   j. Henry Jordan

36. **Between 1921 and 1947 the Packers had just one losing season. What year?**

   a. 1922
   b. 1933
   c. 1944
   d. 1945

37. **In 1974, the Packers acquired the services of quarterback John Hadl, late of the Los Angeles Rams. Those services, as it turned out, didn't add much to the Green Bay team. How many draft picks from the first three rounds did Packers management give up to get him?**

   a. 2
   b. 3
   c. 5
   d. 10

38. **In Super Bowl XXXI, Desmond Howard stunned the Patriots and iced the win for the Packers with a _____-yard kickoff return.**

39. **What team broke the Packers' 25-game home win streak in 1998?**

   _____

40. **Which Boston Red Sox star often attends Packers games? Why?**

   _____

41. **What happened to Charles Martin after he body-slammed Chicago Bears quarterback Jim McMahon onto his bad shoulder, killing the rest of McMahon's season and, some say, the Bears' title chances for 1986?**

    a. He was ejected from the game.
    b. He was ejected from the game and suspended for two more.
    c. He was immediately suspended for the rest of the season.
    d. Nothing.

42. **For two points each, match the player with his nickname.**

    a. Gilbert Brown   f. "The Alabama Antelope"
    b. Reggie White   g. "The Grey Ghost"
    c. Don Hutson   h. "The Gravedigger"
    d. Tony Canadeo   i. "Buckets"
    e. Charles Goldenberg   j. "The Minister of Defense"

43. **What special means of transportation do Packers sometimes use to get to and from the practice field during training camp?**

    a. Green and gold skateboards
    b. A super-stretch Rolls-Royce Silver Cloud
    c. Bicycles belonging to local kids
    d. Unicycles

44. **What Packer fullback, a Hall of Fame member, was suspended for an entire season for gambling?**

    _____

45. **For five points each, give their real first names.**

    a. Curly Lambeau: _____

    b. Fuzzy Thurston: _____

46. Before recordings were used at Lambeau Field, the Green Bay Packer Band provided the musical entertainment. And before that—in the really old days—the stadium's house band was called:

    a. The Lumberjack Band
    b. The Cheese and Chowder Society Marching Band
    c. The Packer Ensemble
    d. The Green and Gold Gang

47. Who was the Packers general manager who acquired Brett Favre?

    R_____ W_____

48. My field goal in the 1965 Western Conference playoff game tied the score over protests by the Colts, who thought the ball went wide. The play allowed us to best the Colts (in overtime, again on the strength of my foot) on our way to the NFL title. Because of the controversy, officials instituted a new rule for field goals calling for a judge under each upright rather than just one in the middle. The rule is informally named after me. Who am I?

    D_____ C_____

49. I came out of the University of Alabama in the pre-draft days. Two teams wanted me, so the league president ruled that whichever one had the paperwork with the earliest postmark could sign me. The Packers won by seventeen minutes. That proved to be good luck for them, as I went on to pretty much invent the category of wide receiver. Who was I?

    D_____ H_____

50. What Pittsburgh Steeler dropped what could have been the match-point touchdown pass in the 1995 Central Division title game?

    _____

51. **What's the family relationship between former Packers Lavvie Dilweg and Anthony Dilweg?**

   a. Father and son
   b. Grandfather and grandson
   c. Brothers
   d. None

52. **Which was *never* a Packers cheerleading group?**

   a. The Packerettes
   b. The Golden Girls
   c. The Green Bay Gals
   d. The Sideliners

53. **What's the name of the fight song played at Lambeau Field every time the Packers score an extra point?**

   " _____ "

54. **Which *isn't* a true statement about Brett Favre?**

   a. His middle name is Lomax.
   b. He grew up in Mississippi.
   c. He's a golfer.
   d. In college, he was injured in a traffic accident and lost 30 inches of his small intestine.
   e. His nickname: "Tailgater."

55. **I'm a former Packer safety who was picked in the same draft as my older brother. (He went to the Baltimore Ravens.) I hope I can be forgiven: After eight Green Bay years, I left the Packers for Minnesota. Who am I?**

   _____

56. They were Green Bay's "Gold Dust Twins," a pair of backs who were paid big bucks in 1965 in hopes that they'd match the achievements of Paul Hornung and Jim Taylor. They didn't. For five points each, who were they?

D_____ A_____

J_____ G_____

57. Two snowy games stand out in Packers history. For five points apiece, name the opposing team in each contest. (For five bonus points each, who won? Another five each for the scores.)

a. November 27, 1977 (six inches of snow during the game):

_____

b. December 1, 1985 ("The Snow Bowl," with nearly eleven inches of snow and howling winds):

_____

58. As is often noted, Green Bay is the smallest city with a major league sports team. Which of these numbers is closest to its population?

a. 52,000   c. 152,000
b. 102,000   d. 202,000

59. Who was Packers head coach when Ron Wolf took over as general manager? (Bonus: Wolf promptly fired him. Who'd he hire to replace him?)

_____

60. The Packers sackmeister is called KGB because few can remember, let alone pronounce, his actual name. Score three points for each of the three parts of the name, with a tenth point for identifying his college (which has *four* parts to *its* name).

K_____ G_____-B_____

_____ _____ _____ University

61. Who played with a broken arm in a game against Detroit in 1963? _____

62. A Packers halfback in the '30s, I was known for leading a fun-filled life off the field, yet I ended up in the Pro Football Hall of Fame. The movie *Leatherheads*, starring George Clooney, more or less tells my life story. I called myself "Johnny Blood." What did my birth certificate call me?

_____

63. It's named after Vince Lombardi. It changes location regularly, usually once a year. It's made of sterling silver. What does it look like, and what's it for?

_____

64. What ex-Packer wide receiver spent two decades providing color with longtime radio man Jim Irwin's play-by-play?

_____

65. The 1989 Packers season was peppered with come-from-behind wins and other close games, which led to this team nickname:

a. "The Catch-Up Gang"   c. "The Breath Holders"
b. "The 'Whew!' Crew"   d. "The Cardiac Pack"

66. One of those '89 games was decided when officials reviewed the tape of Don Majkowski's pass to wide receiver Sterling Sharpe and ruled it acceptable, giving the Packers a win over the Bears. It was their first in five years. By what name does posterity know that game?

a. "The Bears Blow-Out"
b. "The Instant Replay Game"
c. "The Magic and Sterling Show"
d. "Sweet Revenge"

67. I joined the Packers organization from the Cleveland Browns and played defense for Vince Lombardi. During the off-season, I earned an MBA degree, which I put to good use after I retired in 1969. (I own radio stations in the Milwaukee area.) I wore number 87. Who am I?

W_____ D_____

68. In 2005, Vikings wide receiver Randy Moss was fined $10,000 by the NFL for "insulting" treatment of fans as his team handed a playoff defeat to the Packers at Lambeau Field. He said he had only been mocking a Packer fans' tradition. What did he do?

_____

69. The Packers' No. 66, Ray Nitschke, was among the NFL players who appeared with Burt Reynolds in a 1974 movie about a football rivalry between prisoners and their guards. Name that film.

   _____

70. Other wearers of the Green and Gold have had a bit of Hollywood in them. Take, for instance, Brett Favre, Reggie White, and Mike Holmgren, who all appeared in a 1990s football flick. Title, please.

   _____

71. For Green Bay, Donald Driver caught footballs. Earlier, at Alcorn State University, yes, he played football, but he had another sports specialty as well. What was it?

   a. Doubles tennis   c. High jump
   b. Golf   d. Discus

72. For five points each, name the Packer authors of these books:

   a. *Mean on Sunday*: _____

   b. *Instant Replay*: _____

73. After nine years as a Packer cornerback, with two Super Bowl wins, I finished my career with Dallas, where I was part of another Super Bowl victory. But, as I once said, "I'm the only man with a Dallas Cowboys Super Bowl ring who doesn't wear it. I'm a Green Bay Packer." Who am I?

   H_____ A_____

74. Pick the *false* statement about Bart Starr:

   a. The NFL gives a yearly award with his name on it.
   b. He never played college football.
   c. He quarterbacked the Packers to five NFL championships.
   d. He was MVP of the first two Super Bowls.

75. Denver Broncos running back Terrell Davis was a major factor as his team did in Green Bay in Super Bowl XXXII. T.D. rushed for a trio of touchdowns, bringing him MVP honors for the game, despite his sitting out most of the second quarter. What kept him out of play?

   a. Severe leg cramps
   b. Unexplained dizziness
   c. An uncontrollable sneezing fit
   d. A migraine

76. For five points each, what jersey number was shared by:

   a. James Lofton, Jackie Harris, and Derrick Mayes? _____

   b. Willie Wood, Johnnie Gray, and Antuan Edwards? _____

77. In 1974, after four seasons as Packers chief (three of them losers), Dan Devine left for another head coaching position. At that job, he compiled a very healthy 53–16–1 record. With which team?

   a. Washington Redskins
   b. University of Missouri
   c. University of Notre Dame
   d. University of Minnesota

78. Brett Favre isn't the only Packer who couldn't seem to make up his mind about leaving football. Who announced his retirement in April 1998, then changed his mind and did another season with the Packers? (Five bonus points: In 2000, he came back yet again, this time with another NFL team. Which?)

79. Emlen Tunnell spent most of his playing career with the New York Giants, but during his final three years, 1959–61, he wore a Packers uniform. He was noted for his basket-catches—he hauled in punts with his hands held at waist level, like a Willie Mays of the gridiron. His election to the Pro Football Hall of Fame, in 1967, brought him special attention. Why?

_____

80. According to Packers who played on his teams, what's meant by "Lombardi time"?
   a. Show up precisely on time.
   b. Show up early.
   c. Keep your watch on Daylight Time throughout the year.
   d. Keep your watch on Wisconsin time no matter where in the world you are.

81. What record-setting Packer wide receiver retired after the 1994 season because of a congenital spinal condition and became a broadcast analyst, first for ESPN and then for the NFL Network? (Hint: The day before the opening game of what turned out to be his last season, he staged a one-day salary holdout.)

_____

82. What Hall of Fame center did Vince Lombardi trade to the Philadelphia Eagles supposedly because he brought an agent to a meeting with the coach to negotiate for a pay raise?

   J_____ R_____

83. The 1958 season was the Packers' worst ever: 1–10–1. One observer summed it up this way: "The Packers underwhelmed ten opponents, overwhelmed one, and whelmed one." Whose clever line was that?

   a. Sportswriter Red Smith
   b. Comedian Fred Allen
   c. Coach Ray "Scooter" McLean
   d. President Dwight D. Eisenhower

84. In my rookie year as a kicker for the Packers, I helped beat the 49ers in the NFC Championship Game with two field goals and two extra points. Then, in that season's Super Bowl, I kicked a field goal and three extra points but still we lost to Denver. After nine seasons in Green Bay, I signed a free agent contract with the Vikings. Who am I?

   _____

85. What did offensive lineman Keith Uecker do in 1987 that no other Packer did? (Hint: Uecker's fellow Packers were none too happy with him because of it.)

   _____

86. Who, in the tenth game of the 1990 season, was sidelined for the balance of the year when a tackle by Freddie Joe Nunn of the Cardinals tore his rotator cuff? (Nunn drew a personal foul for the play.)

   _____

87. In the 2004 divisional playoff game, after the Philadelphia Eagles bypassed the Green Bay defense to convert a 4th and 26, how did the Eagles march to victory?

_____

_____

88. Which team drafted Brett Favre?

    a. The Baltimore Colts
    b. The Houston Oilers
    c. The Atlanta Falcons
    d. The Tampa Bay Buccaneers

89. I'm a quarterback who in my best year as a Packer tossed the ball for 4,458 yards and 32 touchdowns. In one especially exciting game that year, we carried a scoring contest with the Redskins down to the last seconds, winning it 48–47. Who am I?

_____

90. For many years until Lambeau Field was improved and expanded, a few Packers home games each year were played elsewhere, most notably and most recently at Milwaukee County Stadium. Within two years, what was the last year the Packers played there?

_____

91. What two things from their college playing days do Desmond Howard and Charles Woodson have in common? (Hint: One has to do with where they played, the other with national awards they won.)

_____

_____

92. Why, during the latter part of the 2003 season, did Packers wear a sticker on their helmets with a numeral 3 in a black football?

_____

_____

93. When broadcast play-by-play man Wayne Larrivee decides a game's fate is sealed, he pronounces:

    a. "It's a done deal!"
    b. "Hey hey! Hey hey! Hoo hah!"
    c. "There is your dagger!"
    d. "I smell a MacGuffin!"

94. What radio and TV sportscaster, a former center for Green Bay, has a dislocated pinky from an old game injury?

_____

95. Max McGee, the surprise star of the first Super Bowl, caught seven passes for 138 yards and two touchdowns in that historic game. How many passes had he caught during the season leading up to the championship game?

    a. 4   c. 15
    b. 7   d. 39

96. Why did McGee say he was especially unlikely to perform as well as he did that day?

_____

97. In how many of his 16 seasons as a Packers pitcher did Bart Starr pass for more than 2,500 yards?

_____

98. The first Packer to score five touchdowns in a game: _____

99. What wide receiver tallied 1,497 yards in receptions during the 1995 season?

R_____ B_____

100. Among the handful of jersey numbers retired by the Packers are two consecutive numbers. For five points each, which numbers? (For five bonus points each, whose are they?)

_____

ANSWERS

1. The local newspaper editor who, with Curly Lambeau, co-founded the Packers in 1919

2. b.

3. On January 1, 1967, Green Bay beat Dallas for the 1966 league title; on December 31 of that same year, again facing the Cowboys, the Packers took the title for 1967

4. Ezra Johnson

5. d.

6. Ray ("Scooter") McLean and Ray Rhodes

7. Ray Rhodes held the job between Mike Holmgren and Mike Sherman

8. Mark Brunell

9. LeRoy Butler

10. Robert Brooks (bonus: "Jump in the Stands")

11. c. (Redskins, yes; Giants, no)

12. Let's see: XXXI - II ... that's 29 years

13. b.

14. a.

15. A cheesehead

16. Lynn Dickey (extra points: 15)

17. A man who was not only a star but a Starr: quarterback and later head coach Bart Starr

18. c.

19. Brett Favre's Steakhouse; Fuzzy's #63 Bar & Grill (Fuzzy Thurston)

20. The New York Giants (bonus: 27–0 in 1939, 37–0 in 1961)

21. c.

22. It was a win (bonus: 9–6)

23. d.

24. c.

25. Don Majkowski (bonus: Green Bay beat Cincinnati 24–23)

26. Reggie White

27. Won the NFL championship a third year in a row (1929–30–31 and 1965–66–67)

28. a. 81 yards, b. the Minnesota Vikings

29. b. (Ford, a star center for Michigan, opted instead to coach football and boxing at Yale while trying to get into law school)

30. Clark Hinkle, Ray Nitschke

31. "The Ice Bowl"

32. Ken Bowman and Jerry Kramer

33. e.

34. "The Frozen Tundra"

35. a.-i., b.-g., c.-j., d.-h., e.-f.

36. b.

37. c.

38. 99

39. Minneapolis

40. David "Big Papi" Ortiz, whose wife is a Wisconsinite

41. b.

42. a.-h., b.-j., c.-f., d.-g., e.-i.

43. c.

44. Paul Hornung

45. a. Earl, b. Fred

46. a.

47. Ron Wolf

48. Don Chandler ("The Don Chandler Rule")

49. Don Hutson

50. Yancey Thigpen (thanks, Yance)

51. b.

52. c.

53. "Go! You Packers! Go!"

54. a. (it's Lorenzo)

55. Darren Sharper (brother of Jamie)

56. Donny Anderson and Jim Grabowski

57. a. Vikings 13, Packers 6; b. Packers 21, Buccaneers 0

58. b.

59. Lindy Infante (bonus: Mike Holmgren)

60. Kabeer Gbaja-Biamila, from San Diego State University

61. Ray Nitschke

62. John McNally

63. It's a sterling silver football and it's the Vince Lombardi Trophy, awarded to the team that wins each year's Super Bowl

64. Max McGee

65. d.

66. b.

67. Willie Davis

68. Spoofing the Green Bay tradition of fans mooning the losing team's bus, Moss, after making a fourth-down reception that clinched the Viking victory, pretended to drop trou in the end zone and moon the Packer stands

69. *The Longest Yard*

70. *Reggie's Prayer*

71. c.

72. a. Ray Nitschke, b. Jerry Kramer

73. Herb Adderley

74. b. (he played for University of Alabama)

75. d.

76. a. 80, b. 24

77. c.

78. Reggie White (bonus: the Carolina Panthers)

79. He was the first black player chosen for the Hall of Fame

80. b.

81. Sterling Sharpe

82. Jim Ringo

83. a.

84. Ryan Longwell

85. He crossed the picket line and played with "replacement" players during an NFL players' strike

86. "The Magic Man," Don Majkowski

87. After another first down on the ground, David Akers hit for a 37-yard field goal, forcing a sudden death overtime, in which another Akers field goal squashed Green Bay 20–17

88. c.

89. Lynn Dickey

90. 1994

91. Both played for the University of Michigan Wolverines, and both won the Heisman Trophy and the Walter Camp Award (six years apart, Howard in 1991, Woodson in 1997)

92. To memorialize Tony Canadeo, who had died during the season

93. c.

94. Larry McCarren

95. a.

96. Not expecting to play, he said, he spent the whole night before drinking and suited up next morning nursing a powerful hangover

97. None

98. Paul Hornung

99. Robert Brooks

100. Numbers 14 and 15 (bonus: belonging, permanently, to Don Hutson and Bart Starr)

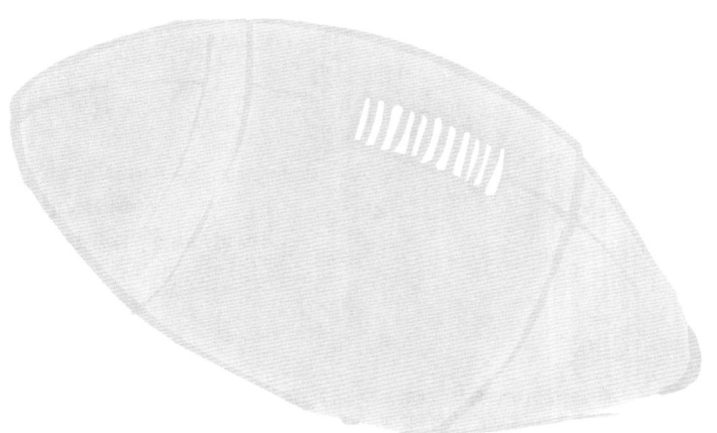